THE HISTORY OF THE **TAMPA BAY BUCCANEERS**

THE HISTORY OF THE
TAMPA BAY

Published by Creative Education
123 South Broad Street
Mankato, Minnesota 56001
Creative Education is an imprint of The Creative Company.

DESIGN AND PRODUCTION BY **EVANSDAY DESIGN**

LIBRARY OF CONGRESS CATALOGING-IN-PUBLICATION DATA

Goodman, Michael E.
The history of the Tampa Bay Buccaneers / by Michael E. Goodman.
p. cm. — (NFL today)
Summary: Traces the history of the team from its beginnings through 2003.
ISBN 1-58341-315-4
1. Tampa Bay Buccaneers (Football team)—History—Juvenile literature.
[1. Tampa Bay Buccaneers (Football team)—History. 2. Football—History.]
I. Title. II. Series.

GV956.T35G64 2004
796.332'64'0975965—dc22   2003060470

First edition

9 8 7 6 5 4 3 2 1

COVER PHOTO: linebacker Derrick Brooks

PHOTOGRAPHS BY
Corbis (Bettmann, Michael Maloney/San Francisco Chronicle, Reuters, UPI/Corbis-Bettmann), Getty Images, SportsChrome USA

HUNDREDS OF YEARS AGO, NATIVE AMERICANS BUILT A SMALL VILLAGE NEAR A BAY ON THE WEST COAST OF FLORIDA. SPANISH EXPLORERS WHO CAME SEARCHING FOR GOLD IN THE EARLY 1500S CALLED THE VILLAGE "TAMPA" AND THE NEARBY BODY OF WATER "TAMPA BAY." THE EXPLORERS WERE NOT THE ONLY GOLD SEEKERS. ACCORDING TO LEGEND, DARING SPANISH PIRATE JOSÉ GASPAR ALSO SAILED ALONG THE COAST NEAR TAMPA BAY, PLUNDERING MERCHANT SHIPS. THE AREA REMAINED UNDEVELOPED UNTIL THE 1880S, WHEN A RAILROAD LINE WAS BUILT LINKING THE "TWIN" TAMPA BAY CITIES OF TAMPA AND ST. PETERSBURG WITH OTHER GROWING AREAS OF NORTHERN FLORIDA. ONCE THE TAMPA BAY REGION WAS OPENED UP, NEW SETTLERS POURED IN. IN 1976, ANOTHER RESIDENT MOVED TO TOWN: AN EXPANSION TEAM IN THE NATIONAL FOOTBALL LEAGUE (NFL). IN HONOR OF THE AREA'S PIRATE LEGENDS, THE NEW FRANCHISE WAS NAMED THE BUCCANEERS.

[Wide receiver Alvin Harper]

TO DIRECT THE first-year Buccaneers, team owner Hugh Culverhouse hired John McKay, one of college football's most successful coaches. McKay had three important qualities—outstanding coaching skills, patience, and a good sense of humor—and he would need them all. Realizing that success in Tampa Bay would not come overnight, McKay once told reporters that he had a five-year plan to make the Bucs great. Why five years? "It's simple," he said. "I had a five-year contract. If I would have had a six-year contract, I would have had a six-year plan."

McKay probably felt like revising his timeline once the club began playing. In 1976, the Buccaneers lost every game, going 0–14. The team continued to struggle the next year even after adding talented running back Ricky Bell. Twelve weeks into the 1977 season, the Bucs' all-time record stood at 0–26. Finally, in the team's 27th game,

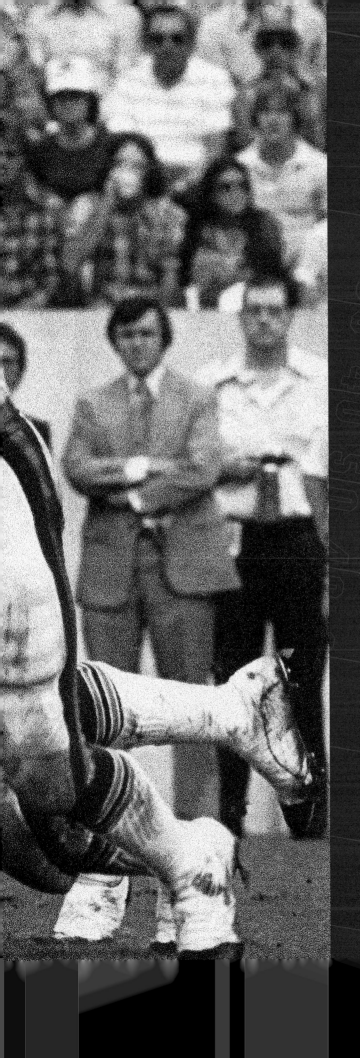

Tampa Bay defenders returned three interceptions for touchdowns to produce a 33–14 triumph over the New Orleans Saints and end the losing streak.

Although Tampa Bay sputtered offensively in its early years, it had a solid defense that featured linemen Dave Pear, Council Rudolph, and Lee Roy Selmon. Selmon, the team's first draft pick in the 1976 NFL Draft, was the heart of the defense. At 6-foot-3 and 255 pounds, Selmon had average size for an NFL defensive tackle, but his talent was anything but average. "During the game, Lee Roy never says a word," said Chicago Bears offensive lineman Ted Albrecht. "He just lines up on every play and comes whirling in like a tornado."

The "Selmon tornado" would continue to whirl through the 1984 season. Then Selmon would help build a strong athletic program at Tampa's University of South Florida. The entire area would celebrate in 1995 when he became the first (and still only) Buccaneers player elected to the Pro Football Hall of Fame.

DOUG WILLIAMS STANDS TALL>

COACH MCKAY BUILT a respectable defense around Selmon and linebacker Richard Wood, and in 1978 he finally found an offensive leader in quarterback Doug Williams. At 6-foot-4 and 215 pounds, Williams had the size and strength to be a pro quarterback. The biggest obstacle he faced was history. Before Williams, there had been few successful African-American quarterbacks in the NFL. Williams challenged those who doubted him. "Race has nothing to do with what I can and cannot do," he said. "The only thing that counts is my performance on the field."

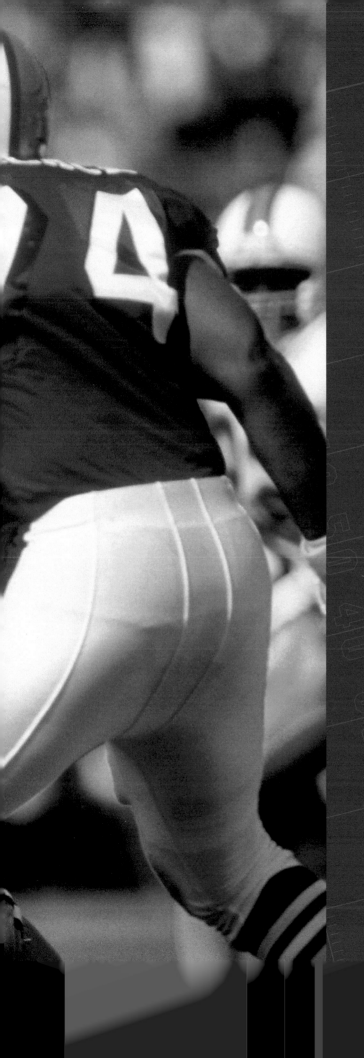

In 1978, the Bucs offense—led by Williams, Bell, wide receiver Morris Owens, and tight end Jimmie Giles—carried the team to a 4–4 start before injuries led to a late-season collapse. In 1979, the club captured its opening game and kept on winning. When the Bucs eked out a 3–0 victory over the Kansas City Chiefs in the last week of the season, they earned both the National Football Conference (NFC) Central Division title and their first playoff berth. Just three years after going 0–14, Tampa Bay had achieved a 10–6 record. Jubilant fans in Tampa Stadium held up banners that read: "From Worst to First."

In the playoffs, Tampa Bay defeated the Philadelphia Eagles 24–17 to reach the NFC championship game against the Los Angeles Rams. A victory would mean a trip to the Super Bowl. The Buccaneers held their own in a tough defensive battle against the Rams but came up short, 9–0.

THE BUCCANEERS DROPPED to 5–10–1 in 1980.

Still, Williams continued to improve, throwing for almost 3,400 yards, with many passes going to rookie receiver Kevin House. The big quarterback was even better in 1981, and with the help of two outstanding rookies—linebacker Hugh Green and running back James Wilder—the Bucs bounced back with a 9–7 record and another division title. But the Bucs were no match for the Dallas Cowboys in the opening round of the playoffs, falling 38–0.

Tampa Bay reached the playoffs again in 1982, but its fortunes fell the next season when Williams left town to join a team in the new United States Football League. Without an experienced quarterback, the Buccaneers dropped to 2–14. The one bright spot was Wilder, who developed into one of the league's best rushers. A tireless

runner, Wilder wanted the ball on every play. "When my number is called," he said, "it's my turn to make things happen."

Wilder led the Bucs in rushing in 1983, despite playing much of the season with broken ribs. Fully recovered the next season, he set an NFL record with 407 carries, gained 1,544 rushing yards, and caught 85 passes. Still, Tampa Bay finished the 1984 season 6–10, prompting Coach McKay to retire. His replacement, Leeman Bennett, confidently told fans, "I expect our team to contend for the NFC Central Division title now, not later."

Unfortunately, bad play and bad luck doomed the Buccaneers throughout the mid-1980s. First, the team plummeted to the bottom of the NFL standings with back-to-back 2–14 seasons in 1985 and 1986, and Coach Bennett was fired. Then, the Buccaneers pinned their hopes for a brighter future on their top choice in the 1986 NFL Draft: super-fast running back Bo Jackson. Jackson, however, decided to play professional baseball instead, leaving the Bucs adrift.

NOTHING SEEMED TO go right in Tampa Bay until 1987.
Then new coach Ray Perkins made two key draft picks
that he hoped would put the club back on the winning
track: University of Miami quarterback Vinny Testaverde,
who had won the 1986 Heisman Trophy as America's top
college player, and speedy receiver Mark Carrier.

In 1988, the Testaverde-to-Carrier connection clicked
for 57 receptions, five touchdowns, and nearly 1,000
yards. That was the good news. The bad news was that
too many of Testaverde's passes were being caught by defenders; his 35 interceptions were a league worst. Perkins
showed patience with his new quarterback, but the fans
didn't and greeted each inaccurate pass with loud boos.
"It's not fun to be me as a football player right now,"
Testaverde admitted. "What would really please me is to
go out and play great. That would shut everybody up."

Testaverde's accuracy improved over the next few seasons, but the team continued to post losing records. In 1992, Coach Perkins was replaced by Sam Wyche, who decided to design the offense around the running of halfback Reggie Cobb. Wyche also decided that Testaverde was not the team's quarterback of the future and released him.

In letting Testaverde go, Coach Wyche seemed to be saying, "We're making a clean break with the past and looking only toward the future." The changes began in 1993 with the addition of rookie defensive end Eric Curry and aggressive linebacker Hardy Nickerson. Wyche continued to shake up the offense in 1994 by drafting quarterback Trent Dilfer and running back Errict Rhett. Both players were soon starters, and Rhett became the first Bucs rookie to rush for more than 1,000 yards.

In 1995, Tampa Bay drafted powerful defensive tackle Warren Sapp. In Sapp, the Buccaneers acquired an angry young star. Although extremely talented, Sapp was falsely rumored to have had drug problems in college and was passed over by several teams in the NFL Draft before Tampa Bay selected him. He promised to repay the team's trust. "The Bucs won't be 26th or 27th in defensive stats anymore," he said confidently. "With me here, there'll be no more numbers like that."

DEFENSIVE WITH DUNGY>

THE REBUILT BUCCANEERS opened the 1995 season 5–2. Then an injury to top receiver Alvin Harper and
poor play by Dilfer led to a total offensive collapse. When
the season ended, the Bucs were a mere 7–9, and Sam
Wyche was fired. His replacement, defensive specialist
Tony Dungy, promised to bring a new winning attitude
to Tampa Bay.

One of Coach Dungy's first moves was to draft fullback
Mike Alstott, a triple-threat runner, receiver, and blocker
from Purdue University. According to college legend, the
powerful Alstott would sometimes train by pushing his
car across parking lots at Purdue. He had one dream in
mind. "The only thing I ever wanted to be was an NFL
player," he said. In 1996, the rookie quickly proved he be-
longed, ranking second on the team in rushing, first in
pass receiving, and number one in bone-jarring blocks.

Star Derrick Brooks made four interceptions in 1999 ^

John Lynch was known for his teeth-rattling tackles ^

Thanks to Sapp, linebackers Hardy Nickerson and Derrick Brooks, and hard-hitting safety John Lynch, Tampa Bay's defense was among the NFL's best in 1997 and set a team record with 44 quarterback sacks. And with shifty running back Warrick Dunn alongside Dilfer and Alstott in the backfield, the club won its first five games and finished the season 10–6, the first winning record in Tampa Bay in 16 years.

In the 1999 season, Coach Dungy's fast-rising Bucs put together an 11–5 record and won the NFC Central Division title. The club's defense was superb in the playoffs as Tampa Bay beat the Washington Redskins 14–13 and then lost an 11–6 thriller to the eventual world champion St. Louis Rams in the NFC championship game.

WITH A STRONG DEFENSE in place, Coach Dungy tried to improve the Bucs' offense by adding wide receiver Keyshawn Johnson in 2000 and quarterback Brad Johnson in 2001. Although the additions made the Bucs a more balanced team, they came up short of the Super Bowl both years. Team owner Malcolm Glazer and general manager Rich McKay grew impatient and fired Dungy.

In February 2002, McKay approached the Oakland Raiders about hiring their coach, Jon Gruden. The Raiders offered to trade away their coach but for a very high price—four draft picks and $8 million. McKay made the deal, and Gruden would prove to be worth the cost. Famous for working 18-hour days, the young and intense coach inspired his players to work harder, too. "Jon brought an intensity and an energy that we needed," said Mike Alstott. "His fire was something we could feed off of."

A brilliant offensive strategist, Jon Gruden was only 38 years old when he became the Bucs' coach.

Under Coach Gruden, the Bucs finished the 2002 season with a franchise-best 12–4 record, captured their first NFC South Division title, and roared into the playoffs for the fourth straight year. This time, there was no stopping them. Tampa Bay crushed the San Francisco 49ers 31–6 and then rolled over the Philadelphia Eagles 27–10 to earn the club's first Super Bowl appearance.

The Super Bowl was expected to be a titanic battle between the NFL's best offensive team, the Raiders, and its best defensive team, the Buccaneers. But the Bucs dominated on both offense and defense, rolling to a decisive 48–21 victory. As the Bucs held the Super Bowl trophy high, both players and fans celebrated a championship 27 years in the making. "To become world champions is the ultimate for any football player," said Brad Johnson, "and I can't even put into words how great it feels."

The Buccaneers were proud of their success but not satisfied with just one title. In the 2003 NFL Draft, the team added defensive end Dewayne White to an already talented defensive line that included end Simeon Rice and tackle Anthony McFarland. The team also used the draft to add Chris Simms, a young passer the team hoped would become the Bucs' quarterback of the future.

For the Tampa Bay Buccaneers and their fans, the voyage from the depths of the NFL to its pinnacle has been a long and rough one. But after finally raising a world championship banner in 2002, today's Bucs plan to add several more and create their own legend in Tampa Bay. In a region with such a colorful past, the Tampa Bay Buccaneers should have a golden future.

INDEX >